Osvaldo Golijov

Oceana

for Vocalist, Boy Soprano,
Chorus and Orchestra

Choral Score

HENDON MUSIC

BOOSEY & HAWKES

AN IMAGEM COMPANY

DISTRIBUTED BY

HAL•LEONARD®
CORPORATION
7777 W. BLUEMOUND RD. P.O. BOX 13819 MILWAUKEE, WI 53213

www.boosey.com
www.halleonard.com

Published by Boosey & Hawkes, Inc.
229 West 28th Street, 11th Floor
New York NY 10001

www.boosey.com

First printed 1996
Second impression with imprint page, 2011
Third impression with new copyright, 2012

Oceana

Texts

Oceana nupcial, cadera de las islas,

Aquí a mi lado, cántame los desaparecidos

Cantares, signos, números del río deseado.

Quiero oir lo invisible, lo que cayó del tiempo

Al palio equinoccial de las palmeras.

Dame el vino secreto que guarda cada sílaba:

Ir y venir de espumas, razas de miel caídas

Al cántaro marino sobre los arrecifes.

Oceana, reclina tu noche en el Castillo

Que aguardó sin cesar pasar tu cabellera

En cada ola que el mar elevaba en el mar

Y luego no eras tú sino el mar que pasaba,

Sino el mar sino el mar

Oceana, dame las conchas del arrecife

Parta cubrir con sus relámpagos los muros,

Los Spondylus, heroes coronados de espinas,

El esplendor morado del murex en su roca:

Tú sabes como sobre la sal ultramarina

En su nave de nieve navega el argonauta.

Oceana, bridal, Oceana, thigh of the islands

Sing to me here, by my side, the vanished

Chants, signs, numbers of the desired river.

I want to hear what is invisible, what fell

From time to the equinoctial mantle of the palm

trees.

Give me the secret wine contained in each syllable

The coming and going of foams, of races of honey

Fallen to the marine jar over the reefs.

Oceana, recline your night in the castle

That awaited forever your mane coming

In each wave that the sea elevated in the sea

And then it wasn't you the one coming

But the sea but the sea

Oceana, give me the shells of the reef

to cover with their lightning the walls

the Spondylus, heros crowned with thorns

the splendor of the murex on the rocks:

You know how, over the ultramarine salt,

In his vessel of snow, the Argonaut sails.

From *Oceana* (In Cantos Ceremoniales)

By Pablo Neruda

OCEANA

1. Call—(chorus tacet)

2. First Wave

Poem by Pablo Neruda

Osvaldo Golijov

4

Interlude

attacca

3. Second Wave

* Altos and Basses: all the cresc. and dim. refer more to intention, direction and intensity than to actual dynamic changes.

12

14

4. Second Call—chorus tacet

nir.

nir

nir.

ir

nir

nir

nir

nir

5. Third Wave

42

44

6. Aria—chorus tacet

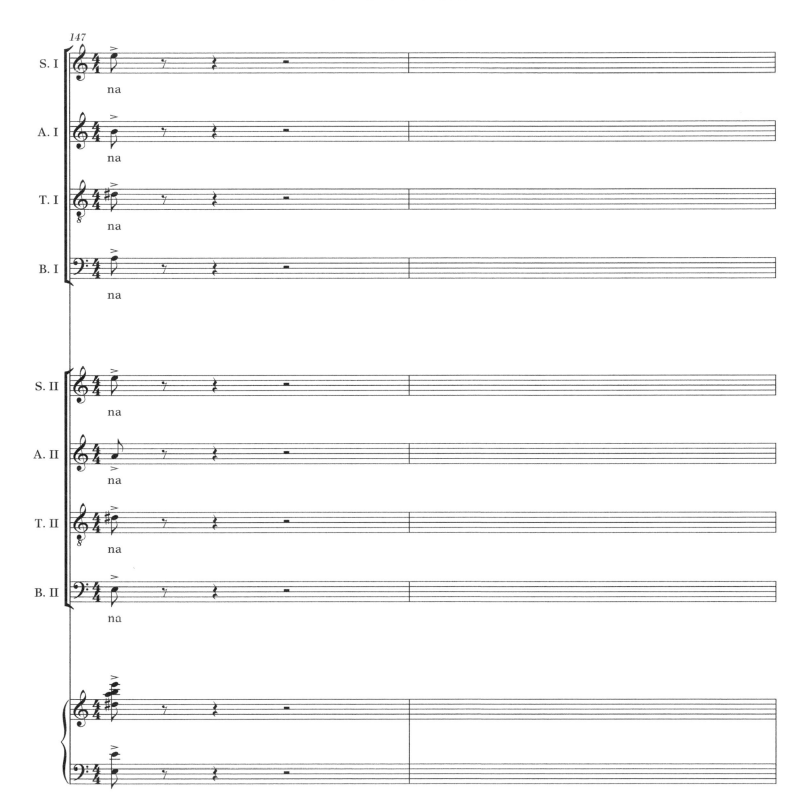

7. Coral del Arrecife
(Chorale of the Reef)

★   The overall effect of this movement should be of a continuous series of gentle waves originating from each choir,
all arriving to lick a single point on a shore. The dynamic variations are fluid and minimal.

The lines (-) on top of certain notes mean subtle emphasis (not quite an accent), as if to provide the energy to carry
the "wave-phrases" those notes originate.

When no articulation markings appear, let the normal "spoken" accent of each word (this is generally shown in the way
groups of notes are beamed) provide the shape to the "wave-phrases".

Most importantly: preserve the liquid substance of the music, especially in making the consonants fluid,
and approach this movement as a prayer to Oceana, the Ocean-Goddess.

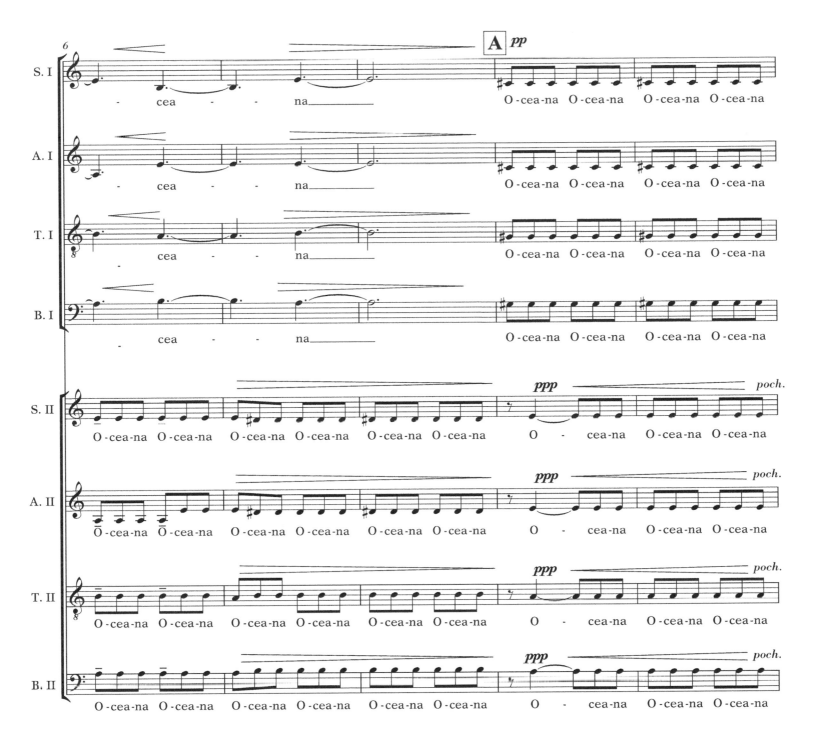

56

58

* Sop I & Alto I: The others join gradually and imperceptibly over the fermata on m. 123.

Poco Meno Mosso